HOW SOCIETIES CHOOSE WEALTH OR POVERTY

AND THE IMPORTANCE OF USEFUL PRODUCTIVITY

Richard Graven

VANTAGE PRESS
New York

To all those whose daily work is useful to society

Contents

Preface

Engineers are those individuals in society who are usually interested in building something of substance. They are interested in complex problems. They are fascinated by science and technology and its application for the use of mankind. Engineers are usually content doing these things. They don't often get involved with politics or speak out on contentious issues. So it is somewhat unusual for an engineer to address a societal issue of some magnitude, namely: "Why do some societies prosper while others fail?"

Many books about society are written by people with an axe to grind. They are upset. They want someone or some entity punished because of an injustice they perceive. This book takes a different tack. It starts with the premise that we have to take mankind as it is, for better or worse and with all its warts, and make the best of it. The challenge is, "How can the efforts of mankind be focused so society will better itself, so the quality of life can be improved, and the environment can be protected?"

A complex question like this can benefit from an engineering approach. Start by examining the basic concepts that govern the behavior of mankind. Then step by step, build upon those concepts and see where it takes us. You may find some of the conclusions surprising and hard medicine to take but they are reality. Mankind has the ability to choose the kind of society it wants to live in. Surprisingly, many opt for poverty. It doesn't have to be this way if you understand what has to be done to choose wealth.

Acknowledgments

My thanks to my fellow chemical engineers, Stanley Dumovich and Dr. Lou Theodore, also graduates of The Cooper Union. Their enthusiasm and encouragement helped me bring this effort to fruition. Also, special thanks to my son, Paul, who gave me valuable assistance during the editing process.

I. Introduction

Winston Churchill once said something to the effect that, "Democracy doesn't work but it's still better than any other system of government." Democracy gives people a voice in their government, it fosters free enterprise, and it allows good and bad ideas to be tried out. But its greatest advantage is that it is dynamic and it can change direction peaceably when it becomes apparent to enough people that change is needed.

Democracy is an evolving system and, in the United States, it has evolved into what one might call "Benevolent Democracy." Because of free enterprise, the United States has become a very wealthy country. Thus, it has been possible for people to look to the government to satisfy needs and desires that they could not obtain by their own efforts. Government has been happy to respond to these requests because these needs have expanded the role, size, and power of government. Many people now look to government as a pseudo-parent to make decisions for them and provide security in terms of their personal needs and comfort as a parent would for a child. Unfortunately, the "child" is getting spoiled and the list of wants and desires keeps growing. The benevolent approach has not been very successful because no problem ever seems to be solved and the size of government and its programs just keeps growing and growing. Benevolent democracy can continue as long as the money holds out. If the money does run out, the impact on law and order in society could be most unpleasant.

The purpose of this treatise is to suggest a change in direction for democracy in the United States so that this system of government will not fail. To this end, I believe that the concept of "Useful Productivity" must become

1

part of the basic foundation of democracy. If this is done, democracy can continue to prosper and there will be the wherewithal to continue to enhance quality of life and to preserve the beauty and variety of life on our planet.

The concept of **"Useful Productivity"** is best understood by first considering some fundamental aspects of human nature and the development of society over the ages. We are all influenced greatly by the past and our culture. As much as we would like to change or be an independent thinker, all of our reasoning is couched in terms of what we know and have experienced. Therefore, if we are to change the future, we must also understand the past.

II. The Evolution of Society

For millions of years, mankind struggled just to survive. Even though the earth was abundant, daily life was fraught with many difficulties and dangers. Much of a day in primitive times was spent gathering food or hunting, providing shelter from the ravages of weather or seeking protection from predators or enemies. Life spans were short.

Mankind became tribal because blood ties were an effective basis for working together to obtain protection or to gain an advantage over others. As knowledge and reasoning powers evolved, some tribes became more proficient than others and advanced their quality of life. This higher quality of life made them subject to attack by other tribes that coveted their advantages.

A major evolution occurred when tribes banded together as a society to gain a numerical advantage over other tribes. A less dominant tribe would sacrifice some rights and wealth to a more dominant tribe in return for protection. This societal arrangement allowed individuals more time to produce items needed for daily survival, and mankind began to produce more than their daily needs. The surplus in excess of daily needs led to bartering whereby an individual could exchange his surplus items for someone else's surplus. Bartering allowed individuals to specialize in producing those goods that were most suitable to their talents. If they could concentrate on producing a surplus of a particular item that others needed, then they had a mechanism to obtain their necessities of life by bartering.

Bartering had its limitations. It might be difficult to find something you wanted in exchange for your surplus. Multiple transactions might be required. There might be a time delay when you were ready to barter but the other person wasn't. So it was logical to find a way to facilitate the barter transaction. That's why money was invented. It made it much easier to swap surplus production based on a common unit of exchange using something valuable. Gold was an ideal medium of exchange. It was limited in supply, it didn't wear out, and people were willing to accept it in exchange for their surplus goods or their services.

Money, in the form of gold, facilitated the growth in power and infrastructure of a society. A society could now pay more easily for government. Government, whether it be led by a king, lord, chief, emperor, or whatever, had the opportunity to increase its power through taxation of its constituency. It was much easier to collect gold than perishable produce or animals. With gold, an army could be bought, weaker societies conquered, and their wealth and land taken. Since gold was a commodity in limited supply, a strong government had the opportunity to initiate an innovation. They minted coins with a likeness of someone powerful on them and required that the constituency use it as legal tender in place of gold. Coins worked well as a medium of exchange to replace bartering as long as too many coins weren't issued and the government was strong. It was only a matter of time before paper money supplemented coins.

Money, like many innovations of mankind, has both a good and a bad side. A negative aspect of money is that it made easy the taxation of the productive accomplishments of the individuals of a society. This source of wealth allowed governments to become powerful and large and engage in wars in search of more wealth, power, and land as well as to subjugate their own citizens and those it conquered. On an individual level, another negative aspect of money is that its universality makes it easy to covet by devious means.

On the positive side, the availability of money as a medium of exchange for the surplus production of individuals has been a key element in facilitating the advancement of society. Money allowed commerce and trade to expand. It allowed science, technology, and the arts to develop where governments provided stability and law and order. It facilitated education of the populace. It allowed the age of knowledge and reason to begin. The productivity of mankind was no longer limited to meeting the needs of basic survival. Man began to create wealth because he was able to begin producing more than was needed to supply just the basic needs of himself and his family.

The Industrial Revolution was born because of the economic incentive to increase the productivity of mankind through the use of machines. Creation of wealth accelerated, but not necessarily fairly. The lot of many people was improved by moving from farming of small plots of land to factory work, but unrest developed because working conditions were bad and workers were paid poorly compared to the wealth amassed by factory owners. This occurred because there was an imbalance between the large supply of potential workers versus the limited availability of factory jobs. Wealth creation had not grown to the point of creating sufficient industry to balance the supply of labor and thereby correct unfair treatment of labor through normal competition. The unfair treatment of this new, specialized labor force led to social unrest and then to experiments with social systems that might be fairer to the laborer or at least punish the rich factory owners.

III. Productivity under Democracy and Socialism

When governments provide stability and allow opportunity to flourish, then the creative and industrious spirit of its population is released to create wealth. Stability requires certain conditions: a currency that holds its value, truth and honesty in transactions, control of crime, defense of the country to prevent war, free trade, and a system of checks and balances to minimize the abuse of power. An educated, middle class population is generally very content in a democratic form of government. Under these circumstances, the middle class has the capability to produce much more than their basic needs for food, shelter, and comfort. Thus they can create and enjoy the benefits of personal wealth. However, a conflict exists and always has between the lowest class (i.e., the poor) and the richer classes. By definition, the poor do not produce sufficiently to meet their basic needs for food, shelter, and comfort. Many poor tend to blame their lot in life, with or without justification, on exploitation by others.

Socialism was a great experiment to improve the lot of the poor by the forced transfer of wealth from the richer classes to the poor. To a great extent, socialism has failed. This is not to be unexpected because:

1. There are never sufficient numbers of rich to cover the income needs of the poor, so the wealth of the middle class must be tapped to meet the need.
2. A large bureaucracy is needed to enforce and allocate the transfer of wealth. Since it is difficult to establish a system of checks and balances for

a large bureaucracy, inefficiency and incompetency soon prevail, leading to enormous waste.

3. An incentive is created for individuals to rely on wealth created by others rather than personal work with the outcome that the number of poor people increases dramatically as well as the size of the bureaucracy needed to administer wealth transfer.

4. It is impossible to maintain honesty and avoid fraud when tremendous amounts of wealth are being transferred, so a lack of respect for law and order develops with the erosion of honor and trust.

5. There is a negative effect on education because the young are guaranteed a future income regardless of their skill or knowledge.

6. A loss of self-esteem occurs for individuals receiving benefits, which is accompanied by a loss in feeling of responsibility for others or responsibility for one's own actions.

7. The incentive to expend extra effort to create wealth is diminished when there is insufficient reward for the extra effort expended. In other words, why work hard if everybody gets the same pay regardless of accomplishment or why work hard if the fruits of one's labors are almost confiscated by excessive taxation?

8. New wealth creation is lessened because capital funds needed to create new business enterprises are diminished by wealth transfer.

9. Disharmony in society increases because the rich and middle class do not like to give up wealth earned by hard work for transfer to others while the poor and those in the bureaucracy

involved in wealth transfer become a large political force whose goal is to increase the transfer.

The saddest example of the result of forced wealth transfer is the most virulent form of socialism, namely Soviet Communism. This form of socialism was based on the utopian concept that mankind was idealistic and a society could be established whereby each individual would produce voluntarily up to his ability, then turn the results of his efforts over to society but receive in return only what he might need to be comfortable. This concept was, of course, contrary to human nature. Mankind needs an incentive to be productive. Those who resisted giving up their wealth, particularly their land, were killed by socialist tyrants. This was a natural outcome as described by Friedrich A. Hayek in his 1944 book *The Road to Serfdom*. Those who were more skilled were resented and killed as well as those who complained. Productivity fell dramatically. All niceties, such as concern for the environment, human rights, improving the infrastructure, etc., fell by the wayside because there were no capital funds to spare in the declining economy. Even though the Soviet experiment was a failure, it will be generations before their society can recover due to the murder of tens of millions of their more talented citizens who would not knuckle down under this tyrannical system.

In hindsight, one wonders why it was not obvious to more people that the Communist experiment would fail. It would seem that people were blindsided by a hatred or envy of those with wealth and power, engendered by the actions of an incompetent czar and a naive belief in an idealist concept that was contrary to the nature of mankind. History has shown us many examples that when hatred is the basis for action by a society, the outcome is not what is expected and often self-destruction occurs and misery for many, particularly the innocent. Although mankind has the capability to apply reason, logic, good sense, and wisdom to improve his lot, it seems that, collectively, the best path for a society cannot be ascertained except by trying all options, however foolish some options might be until, by experience, mankind learns what works and does not work. This trial-and-error approach in the evolution of society is, of course, painful and slow, but it seems to be the only way mankind as a whole can advance. In general, it appears that it is a **natural law: "Mankind (i.e., society) learns by experience, not by reason."**

IV. The Concept of Useful Productivity

An individual begins to create wealth when he or she produces, by useful work, more than that which is required for the basic needs for survival. **The wealth of the society, in which the individual resides, is the sum of the wealth of each of the society's individuals.** This wealth, created by productive individuals, forms the basis for a society's standard of living and quality of life. No society, however well meaning, can solve social, population, environmental or economic problems without the availability of wealth created by its individuals.

The productivity of the individual must be **useful** to produce wealth. **Useful Productivity** means that an individual does useful work to produce some goods or services that someone else deems worthwhile and is willing to buy **voluntarily** with money or to exchange it (i.e., by barter) for a good or service representing someone else's own production or labor. **Useful Productivity** can also be defined as the ability of individuals to provide a product or service that is needed by society and that will improve quality of life.

Useful work creates wealth whereas non-useful work does not create and even destroys wealth. Non-useful work is work that no one would **voluntarily** pay for or exchange for their own useful productivity. For example, suppose a farmer grows tomatoes and he produces a surplus of 1,000 bushels that he wants to sell to buy things his family needs. If the farmer gets $10 for each of his 1,000 bushels, he creates $10,000 of wealth and can buy things he needs with his wealth thus creating demand. His **useful productivity** created wealth. He would not

10

like to barter some of his tomatoes with someone doing useless work or no work because that person has created nothing that has value to the farmer. If the farmer is forced to give his surplus tomatoes to the person doing useless work, his incentive to grow surplus tomatoes is diminished and the value of the tomatoes and their potential wealth creation is diminished.

When the farmer sells the result of his useful productivity, he is, in essence, trading his useful productivity for someone else's useful productivity. Money is helpful to make this trade, but money itself always represents someone's **useful productivity.** When we accept money in exchange for the goods and services that we produce, we are accepting an I.O.U. that someone in the future will give a product or service we want for the money we accepted. It is a **natural law: "The wealth of a society is derived from the sum of the useful productivity of each of its individuals."**

V. A Comment on Money and Deficits

A stable currency is one in which money supply grows only proportionately to the increase in society's **useful productivity.** If a society creates money faster than the increase in useful productivity, then a useful producer wouldn't value money as highly and would demand more for his products or services. The result is inflation or loss in value of money. If the contrary occurs and money supply does not increase as fast as useful productivity, then money becomes more valuable and deflation is said to occur.

There are other factors, of course, which can affect the stability of money. For example, if another society values the stability of the first society's money (say dollars) more than its own, it might be willing to exchange its own currency (i.e., goods) for dollars and then loan the dollars back to the first society in exchange for interest payments. Dollars are created to handle this debt. A problem only arises if the lender gets nervous and becomes unwilling to continue to hold a dollar debt. Then borrowed dollars would flow back to the issuing country and become a call on the goods and services represented by dollars and inflation would result. Many countries have large foreign debts, and this creates a potential for very large inflation risk for these countries if their economies were to falter and there was a loss in confidence in their currency.

VI. What Amount of Money Does a Person Deserve for His or Her Work?

If the farmer in our earlier example had a neighboring farmer who could produce twice as many surplus bushels of tomatoes in a week and sell (or barter) them, no one would deny that the second farmer was entitled to twice as much income. Since the second farmer is adding twice as much wealth to the economy, he is entitled to twice as much benefit. In an ideal society, we can draw the conclusion that remuneration or the amount of money earned for **useful productivity** should be in direct proportion to the quantity and the value of work added to a product or service by the individual doing useful work.

VII. The Value of Useful Productivity

It is not obvious to most people that **useful productivity** is the basis for wealth creation in society. There is a feeling by many, that if the government creates jobs, whether useful or not, then the country will prosper. There is also a feeling that we must not let business get more efficient or adopt new technologies since this will lose jobs and hurt the economy. Although, individuals involved in a job loss are hurt until they can find a new job, the perpetuation of useless or unnecessary jobs does not create wealth but, in fact, diminishes the wealth of the society. The extreme example would be if the government printed money to give everybody an income but nobody did any useful work. Everyone would have money, but there would be nothing to buy. No one would produce beyond what they personally required for survival. Certainly, the farmer in our example would not produce tomatoes for sale if his only return was money that was useless to buy anything. On the other hand, when individual productivity is maximized, the wealth of society is maximized so there are more funds available to create new jobs or that can be tapped for social, environmental, or economic goals that will improve the quality of life for all individuals.

It should be noted that the question of artificial job creation can be a valid issue when large numbers of people are out of work. There is a place for job creation by government as a temporary expedient, particularly if the jobs are useful and contribute to society. However, when there is unemployment, the real problem may be due to a lack of skills by an individual to do available work, the lack of available capital or too high a risk to make a capital investment relative to the return expected. If these are the real problems, then artificial job creation is not a solution.

When wealth creation occurs in a society due to a preponderance of **useful productivity** by the society's individuals and there is stability in society (i.e., stable currency, lack of war, law and order, etc.), then the fruits of knowledge and creativity can flourish to accelerate the creation of more wealth. Science, technology, and craftsmanship can expand to create the means to more efficiently use available resources and thereby make skilled people more productive.

Job creation requires capital (i.e., money) to build facilities or provide the tools that any new job requires. Capital funds only can come from wealth creation by someone. Obviously, people or new businesses have to either self-accumulate or borrow money from someone to get the capital funds needed to start a new venture or business. The interest rate they would have to pay for borrowed funds would depend on two factors : 1) the availability of wealth in the society and 2) the risk the lender might be taking in terms of getting his money back some day, adjusted for expected inflation. The more wealth a society creates and the more people save, the more capital funds are available and the lower the interest rate will be for launching new businesses and creating new, productive jobs. Also, it is only when a society begins to create excess wealth that attention can be given to enhancing the quality of life by protecting the environment, preserving the beauty of nature, and enhancing the beauty and quality of things mankind builds. It is a **natural law: The creation of wealth creates a demand for jobs and makes it possible to protect and enhance the environment.**

Creation of wealth produces surplus money that can be invested to create new jobs or it can be dissipated by waste or foolish use. It is in society's interest that most surplus money be invested into tangible opportunities that have a high probability of being economically sound and generating a profit and thereby creating jobs. Profits from business fuel the wealth-creation engine, leading to more surplus money, which, in turn, allows a business to expand or the creation of new businesses.

How do businesses succeed? When a new business or endeavor is started by a private enterprise, most of the initial funding monies are used for capital expenditures. By capital expenditures, we mean the up-front cost to build a factory or building and install machines or equipment that will allow the endeavor to begin producing income through sales. Thus, a capital expenditure is something of lasting, tangible value. Before spending capital monies, an economic analysis is made to calculate whether the endeavor will generate revenue sufficient to pay off the capital investment in a reasonable time and then generate a profit.

There are many sophisticated ways to make an economic analysis, such as discounted cash flow rate of return or present value calculations, but suffice it to say that private enterprise has a pretty good system to guide it in making investments that make good economic sense. Thus, the important point is that when surplus money created by the useful productivity of society is invested by private enterprise, it is usually invested wisely and creates new, long-lasting jobs that lead to additional wealth creation.

However, in the United States, only about half, or less, of the surplus money created by useful productivity goes into the private sector for investment. The other half flows into the government via taxation. Much of what government does is essential for the functioning of an orderly society, so there is no debate that a government must raise funds by taxation to allow it to function. The critical question is how much does government need, are the funds being spent wisely, and do they contribute to the useful productivity of society? Unfortunately, there is little information to quantitatively assess the extent to which government spends taxpayer money wisely. Government makes no distinction between the money that it spends for capital expenditures and daily operating expenses. It makes no estimate of impact of its expenditures on useful productivity. Its economic calculations, when made, are rarely objective since there is no penalty if they are wrong. Government expenditures are decided principally by prioritizing a list of ways to spend money within a budget that is established by Congress and the President. Since there is no objective way to measure the benefit of government expenditures on the useful productivity of society, one can only speculate. Are we getting no more than thirty cents out of a dollar being spent effectively? That would be my guess. Can someone prove otherwise?

The key point is that surplus funds generated by the useful productivity of a society are limited. For a society to prosper, these funds must be used wisely. Most of these funds should flow to capital investments that will generate wealth or maintain and enhance quality of life. There is never enough money to invest in all the opportunities available, to correct all the things that need to be done, or to solve all of society's problems. A prospering society will begin to falter if it diverts too much of its available surplus money to expenditures that do not generate wealth.

17

Also, a developing society can never escape poverty unless it obtains capital funds through self-generation or loans and these funds are used wisely and not wasted.

VIII. The Impact of Self-Esteem on Productivity

It is an erroneous assumption that everybody's goal in life is just to make money. Obviously, everyone wants to make or get enough money to take care of basic needs like food, shelter, comfort, etc. However, the most compelling drive in mankind appears to be the need to achieve self-esteem and self-respect. Most people want to accomplish something that they or others value or they can be proud of. This can be many things. For some people it is power over others, for some it is money, for some it is a sport trophy, but for most it may be the satisfaction from accomplishing something useful in their work or avocation or helping in the care of others.

People can develop self-esteem by doing good or evil. Obviously, it is in society's interest that individuals be channeled into doing good things. How may we establish an environment where individuals become productive citizens? Probably the most important factor is to be conceived and grow up in a home where a child is loved and nurtured. After all, children are born without knowledge and wisdom. Their consciousness of right and wrong must be turned on by love and training. Knowledge must be imparted by education. Wisdom must be sought from life's experiences and the lessons of the past. Without that type of environment, a child gains little respect for or consideration of others or respect for property. It seems to be **a natural law: "Children are born without wisdom or knowledge. Knowledge can be taught, but wisdom must be sought."**

Under the great, failed socialist experiments to eliminate poverty, the United States has vast numbers of people on welfare. Men, who father children, lose self-esteem because welfare mothers don't need or want a husband around. Illegitimate children frequently do not have a suitable environment in which they can be loved, nurtured, develop self-esteem, and benefit from the wisdom and experience of their elders. Illegitimate children are the most likely not to be receptive to an education in which they will develop a skill that will lead to productive employment and self-esteem from society. Current law helps dictate this outcome. A minimum wage comes nowhere near to matching the amount of money and benefits a single mother can receive on welfare. But the poor and needy must be helped. What are the solutions?

First is the important awareness that everyone has an obligation to make a contribution to society if they want to receive help from society. Then, if they need assistance, the individual still has self-esteem because assistance is no longer just a handout. Secondly, there must always be an incentive to work, no matter how small the salary or simple the job. The only requirement is that the job be something worthwhile, something society needs, and in which doing a good job is important. If an individual will do useful work, then society should be willing to supplement that person's pay on a sliding scale so that there is always the incentive to better one's pay and contribution. The educational system must recognize that it is their job to educate individuals according to their abilities and that everyone must learn a skill that will allow them to do useful work. A high school diploma or a college diploma means nothing if the individual does not graduate with skills that will allow them to produce useful work. When students are taught up to their potential, some will have the gift to learn faster and do complex work more easily than others. It is important that students be taught tolerance for differences in learning abilities as well as humility for any inherent skill advantage they may have. It is particularly in a society's self-interest to educate the most talented to their full capabilities because these are the individuals who are the most likely to create new concepts, new ideas, new jobs and new industries.

It is also in society's self-interest and for the sake of children that laws should favor a commitment to marriage and recognize the importance of fathers in the raising of children. Also, the law should recognize how difficult it is on mothers who are raising children; it is not an easy job. Many mothers look for some escape through work or clubs so that they are not always confined to the job of raising their children on a twenty-four-hour-a-day basis. But children are the future of any society. If their upbringing and education can be effective to impart useful knowledge and ethical principles, it is the best investment a society can make. Every effort should be taken to build incentives for marriage and to reduce illegitimacy. If through illegitimacy, an individual chooses a course in life where they will be dependent on society, rather than contribute useful productivity, they are stealing the wealth of society and diminishing the potential standard of living for everyone. The poor are hurt most when the wealth of society is diminished: less money is available for social programs and less money is available as capital funds to create new jobs.

IX. The Societal Contract

Useful Productivity is so important to the well-being of society and to each individual in it, that we should consider a formal procedure or ceremony whereby individuals would enter into a contract with society. This ceremony could take place when an individual entered an appropriate grade in public or private schools and with the oversight of the parents. In essence, the contract would be:

1. Society (i.e., government, its citizens and parents) agrees to help educate each individual so they will have knowledge and a useful skill in order that the individual can do useful work and accumulate wealth, receive protection from society for problems not of their own doing, and enjoy the benefits of society. In return,
2. The individual agrees to accept a responsibility to society to learn useful skills and to perform useful work within his or her abilities, which will result in useful productivity for their own and society's benefit. The individual acknowledges that the right to receive benefits from government is relinquished if the individual refuses to make a useful contribution to society within their capabilities.

It is vital to convey to every individual the importance of making a contribution to society through **useful productivity.** If we expect something from society, we must be willing to make a contribution to society. We can

22

make that contribution, however small or large, by having a skill that will allow us to do something that will be lawfully useful to others.

X. The Importance of Checks and Balances

There are two great perpetuators of useless work: **monopolies** and **the lack of checks and balances.** There has never been a monopoly that has not become inefficient. If a certain market is guaranteed to an enterprise, there never has been a mechanism devised by mankind to keep that operation efficient. Rate-setting oversight never guarantees that workers or management will be competent. In fact, competent workers or leaders become a threat to incompetent ones. The only thing that avoids the inefficiency and incompetency inherent in monopolies is competition in a free market place. Government is inefficient because it is a monopoly. However, we need government to write laws, provide oversight, maintain law and order, maintain national defense, etc. Government performs best when it leaves as many tasks as possible to private enterprise and allows competition in each area. Wherever possible, government should make the cost of any service that it provides self-supporting by the individuals or organizations that benefit from the service provided. If the service can't be made self-supporting, perhaps the service is not justified.

The nature of mankind is to seek power as a means of seeking self-esteem or to obtain wealth. Power, without checks and balances, leads to corruption. It is admirable of the founding fathers of the United States that they foresaw the need in the Constitution for a strong system of checks and balances. Where there is a lack of checks and balances, both in government and private industry or any aspect of life, inefficiency and diversion of money to selfish interests takes place.

XI. The United States Since World War II

The United States enjoyed great prosperity after World War II. It was the only large industrial country in the world whose physical plant was not destroyed by war. There was a tremendous, pent-up demand for goods, which the U.S. supplied to itself and the rest of the world. The U.S. also had a well-trained labor force and a modest size government so that most of the wealth generated by industrial production went into new industrial or commercial facilities and job creation. The U.S. was also blessed with people of high creativity and innovativeness that led to the development of many new products and industries. It was a period of high employment and burgeoning industrial might.

However, wealth did not always flow fairly into the population. As always, some people gained wealth by exploiting others whereas those exploited were underpaid for their work. Nevertheless, the middle class expanded in numbers and wealth. Given the strength of the economy, it became feasible to inaugurate many expensive social programs based on wealth transfer. Labor unions were strong and were able to drive up manufacturing wages because there was little overseas competition. After decades of prosperity, the public began to assume that prosperity, a comfortable wage, and a broad range of social programs was a guaranteed right.

Unfortunately, all societies in history that become prosperous because of prodigious, useful productivity, eventually fall into the same trap. Prosperity has never lasted because transfer of wealth from workers to non-workers squandered wealth and the society became less

25

productive and often decadent. Unfortunately, much of the public and government in the U.S. are under the assumption that prosperity is automatic and not something that has to be nurtured.

When a society prospers, politicians can offer benefits to their constituents and to special interests, using wealth transfer as a means of funding the benefit. U.S. voters have embraced wealth transfer as a means of enjoying benefits much beyond that possible for the income that they earn. They continue to elect politicians who offer the best "free lunch." These "free lunch" benefits actually have come at a very high price.

In order to administer wealth transfer social programs, the U.S. government has become very large, bureaucratic, and inefficient. Wealth transfer programs have become enormous in size. The cost of these programs and the cost of the government to run them is huge. The concept sold to the electorate initially was that costs would be modest and that the rich would pay for these programs. But the costs are not modest and there are not enough rich. The main burden to pay for these programs has fallen on the middle-class worker. Tax rates are high, but there is still not enough tax revenue to pay for these programs. Government usually learns that at some point, raising tax rates more does not produce more tax revenues because the higher tax rates suppress business activity and therefore total tax revenue is reduced rather than increased. When the tax revenues were insufficient to pay for promised programs, the government resorted to borrowing enormous sums of money to pay for the shortfall in funding of the wealth-transfer programs.

Because of the debt and the ever-escalating cost of wealth-transfer programs, other important things are not being done for the good of society. For example, the maintenance and enhancement of infrastructure that is vital to the future health of the U.S. economy has been allowed to lapse. Existing roads, bridges, waterways, and harbors have been allowed to decline. Important centers of commerce in the U.S. are not being improved to make them more efficient and to reduce the cost of transporting goods. Cities and their infrastructures are decaying.

Since wealth transfer provides a guaranteed income to those in need, there has been a marked decrease on the part of many students and their parents to put value on a good education. Wealth transfer has created a lack of interest and desire to do hard work and accept the discipline that is necessary to become a knowledgeable, responsible, and work-skilled adult. This attitude has led to the marked decline in the elementary and high school educational system in the United States. Knowledge and skill are no longer valued. The smarter students and those who work hard in school are often ridiculed. The pool of skilled, well-educated graduates is falling since a good education is no longer valued by a large percentage of the population.

A disturbing statistic is that 50 percent of the adult population in the U.S. pay only 5 percent of the income taxes collected. The other 50 percent pay 95 percent of the taxes. The percentage paying little or no tax is escalating. Will politicians appeal to this group by larger and larger wealth transfer programs? Will taxpayers become disenfranchised by non-taxpayers?

While this has been transpiring, much of the rest of the world (particularly Asia and South America) has been building up their infrastructure, their educational system, and their industrial capability. Their workers are willing to work for low wages in order to improve their lot in life. More and more low technology U.S. manufacturing plants, whose workers received relatively high pay, could no longer compete with those foreign plants with modern facilities and lower paid workers. U.S. companies, rather than totally lose a business, began to shift production to the lower manufacturing cost, overseas plants, resulting in a loss of jobs for U.S. workers. Today, the U.S. faces a terrible dilemma: how to provide good paying jobs for a large percentage of its population when there has been a tremendous loss in the manufacturing base. U.S. workers obviously do not want to accept a wage scale like those in developing countries. But few displaced, older workers can develop the higher technology skills that would permit them to maintain the wages they are accustomed to. Proposed solutions to this loss in jobs range from establishing protective tariffs to further increases in the transfer of wealth. Neither of these proposed actions will work because they do nothing to solve the basic problem, which is to increase the wealth-generating capacity of the country by increasing useful productivity and to adjust wage scales commensurate with the value added by labor in a worldwide competitive market.

There is a place for trade restrictions when unfair trade practices exist, such as "dumping," or when a foreign government subsidizes its manufacturing plants to take away a market or when they unilaterally block the imports of goods. The wholesale use of restrictive tariffs by the U.S., however, would cut off the flow of lower price imports and substantially raise the cost of living for the U.S. population, thus putting more stress on the income needed by a worker to survive. In addition, if the U.S. instituted protective tariffs, the countries affected would retaliate by instituting tariffs against the import of U.S.

goods. World trade would diminish and a recession would occur just as it did in 1930 with the enactment of the Hawley-Smoot Tariff Act.

Many societies have used trade and tariff barriers to protect their industries whose cost of producing products was non-competitive with other societies. History has shown that trade barriers are not a long-term solution. There is still the feeling that tariff and trade barriers are an answer to non-competitiveness. A tariff is a transfer of wealth; it is a subsidy; it does not enhance the wealth of the society.

The U.S. cannot escape the emergence of other countries as competitors in the marketplace. What it can do is recognize that higher wages can only be sustained by having industries that are more creative and more efficient, which protect their technology, and which can call on skilled and productive workers. Unfortunately, there is no longer the "free lunch" that existed after World War II. Workers in the U.S. are now competing against many others in the world with equal or better skills and comparable equipment.

It is natural in the world for another society to try to improve itself. When a society can attract some capital to build manufacturing plants and its population has some skills and is willing to work for lower wages so they can accumulate some wealth beyond their need for subsistence, should their endeavor be encouraged or discouraged? If it is encouraged, they will begin building wealth in their society, which in turn creates more job demand and eventually a higher standard of living and higher wages. Their growth will lead to demand for products outside their own society and a leveraging up effect for everyone. If we discourage them by tariffs or boycotts, we condemn them to a lower standard of living and hurt ourselves as well. How many wars have been fought because one country limited the ability of other countries to prosper or was envied by others? If we want the world to be a better place, we should be aware of the **natural law: "To enhance my own life, I must enhance the life of others."**

XII. The Problem of Fair Pay for Useful Productivity

In an ideal society, everyone would do useful work. Their remuneration or pay for useful productivity would be in exact proportion to their useful productivity contribution. It would be the equivalent of what they could obtain by barter if money were not the medium of exchange. In our real society, not everyone does useful work and compensation for work is not necessarily in proportion to one's useful productivity; it can be greater or less.

In our earlier example of the farmer, his reward is clear. If he can personally produce a thousand bushels of tomatoes, then he should be entitled to keep whatever he can get for them after deducting his costs and his taxes. Similarly, few would argue that an artist should not keep what he can get for selling an object of art that he created minus costs and taxes. The same goes for an athlete or performer. But in the world of commerce and government, the question of what is fair remuneration is much tougher.

When there is a lack of checks and balances, individuals and organizations can take advantage of others and take a much bigger piece of the wealth pie than they are entitled to by virtue of their own contribution to useful productivity. The ire of workers has always been aroused when they see this happening as they know that part of the fruits of their labors are being taken away from them unfairly. What are some of the areas where there is concern over apparent, unwarranted remuneration? Categories that are prone to abuse are business management, government, unions, and special interests. Also, theft and dishonesty are the way in which some people get an income. This category is growing rapidly, and it has the worst impact on reducing the standard of living and the quality of life for society.

XIII. Abuses Because of the Lack of Checks and Balances

1. Business

Business corporations and enterprises are vital institutions throughout the world because they are an effective means to allow individuals to perform useful productivity and to generate wealth. These organizations can be models of efficiency at satisfying a public need. They bring together people skilled in every needed task to work together as a team to produce ever-improving products that contribute to an ever-growing standard of living. Workers in responsible companies are usually paid wages in line with a competitive job market. That is, skilled workers with more experience command a higher wage than others with less skills or experience. Individual workers who make an exemplary contribution to a corporation's profitability or competitiveness usually receive extra wages. So, in general, corporations have a system in place that is reasonably fair in rewarding workers for their useful productivity.

Businesses are very important to society, and they have great freedom to act as the marketplace may dictate. There is an area of abuse, however, and that is the great growth in the remuneration given to the heads of large corporations, which, in some cases, is far and above the contribution they make to the useful productivity of the corporation. This is viewed as unfair in U.S. society and is a cause of unrest. Out-of-line remuneration for some heads of corporations occurs because there is essentially no check and balance in place. As it is said, "The foxes are guarding the henhouse." Stockholders should have the power to approve this remuneration, but their only ordinary option in the U.S. is either to approve or not approve a slate of officers presented to them. Stockholders do not have a simple way to act in their self-interests if the corporate executives pay themselves too much. This lack of a check and balance could be solved by giving stockholders the statutory obligation to approve the remuneration package for the top executive of a corporation. A few disapprovals would do marvels in making managements in all corporations more accountable for their performance and remuneration and for the corporation's performance.

On the other hand, entrepreneurs are a vital factor in business because they are the ones who will risk capital to start a business with the hope of being successful and earning a worthwhile reward. Small businesses started by entrepreneurs are a major source of new jobs in a society. These entrepreneurs are entitled probably more than anyone to benefit from the enterprises that they create since they risk so much in trying to create a new enterprise. They are entitled to a full reward for their efforts, providing they are not unjustly and illegally exploiting their workers.

2. Government

Government is a monopoly, so it is difficult to establish any effective incentive for government or its workers to be efficient. In the United States, there is no limitation on how much money the government can spend other than that which it can raise by taxation or borrowing. Fortunately, the government does have many effective and hard-working people and does perform many vital functions. Nevertheless, many people in government are doing very little useful work and contributing very little useful productivity to the economy. Their pay, with benefits, tends to be higher than similar workers in the private sector. There is little incentive to dismiss or reassign incompetent government employees. Incompetency in government constitutes a very large waste of wealth of the country, which thereby brings down the standard of living of all productive workers who must support an inefficient government behemoth. Ordinary taxpayers have little or no redress and voice on how much their government can spend. A check and balance is sorely needed so taxpayers have some approval of spending. Perhaps it is time that thought be given to letting taxpayers endorse or reject aspects of the federal budget, say at annual election times, particularly with regard to new spending programs. Also, it is vital that there be a better mechanism in place in government so individuals who are incompetent for the positions that they hold may be transferred or terminated. This also applies to managers and supervisors who are unwilling or unable to be accountable for the poor performance of the people they are supposed to supervise.

3. Lawyers

The practice of law is an important profession that is needed in the world. The aim of the legal profession should be to help individuals, businesses, and governments to **avoid** problems and to help adjudicate disputes. But many lawyers in the United States have a different mission. Their mission is to create problems so as to increase their fees and to seek judgments against any institution with money. By these means, these lawyers command much more of the wealth pie than their efforts justify. In fact, many instances can be shown where their efforts decrease useful productivity and society's wealth. This comes about because of a conflict of interest without checks and balances. The conflict of interest is that the majority of legislators in government are lawyers and they write the laws under which other lawyers function. Today, lawyers are one of the most powerful special interest groups in the United States.

For example, they argue that litigation against corporations and assessing high, punitive judgments are the only way to correct negligent behavior of a corporation. This approach has the effect of taking away capital funds that the corporation may need for expansion or modernization and, in essence, punishing workers who may have nothing to do with the instance of negligence. If there are individuals who are deliberately negligent in a corporation so as to cause harm to the public, then these people should be fined or jailed instead of sacking the resources of the corporation with punitive judgment awards. The tactics of lawyers have brought dishonor to a noble profession. The practice of law should have the intent to help improve the useful productivity of society. Instead it has the flavor of trying to rob society. This abuse might be corrected, if constitutionally, lawyers were barred from being legislators. From a practical standpoint, this won't happen. But, at least, voters should be aware of this conflict of interest and exercise more care and judgment before electing a lawyer to the legislature.

4. Unions

Unions are another institution that serves an important need for those workers who cannot otherwise find an adequate mechanism to address their grievances or who do not receive pay commensurate with prevailing competitive wages for the same work. A union abuses its position, however, when it can strike an organization that is a monopoly that is vital to the public interest. In these cases, the power of the union is very great and instead of merely addressing bona fide grievances of workers, the prime mission of the union becomes one of unbridled power to increase salaries and benefits above a competitive wage, to resist improvements, to expand nepotism, and allow incompetency and inefficiency to continue in the organization. This degree of power is not in a labor union's best long-term interest because its actions tend to make the cost and the inefficiency of the monopoly organization so repugnant to the public that drastic measures will ensue eventually. Society needs organizations that are competent and efficient if useful productivity and the wealth of the society is to be increased. It is totally contrary to the interest of society when a union makes it impossible to replace incompetent workers or makes it all but impossible to make changes that would improve efficiency and reduce the cost of manufacturing or services.

Criticism can also be levied against unions in competitive industries because of the special interest favors they receive from Congress, which allow union leaders to act contrary to the wishes of employees. Nevertheless, there are the checks and balances in that if the union imposes demands that are too unreasonable, their industry is put in jeopardy of failure because of competition from non-union firms or industry outside of the United States. Most unions in competitive industries are enlightened enough not to go so far as to put their employer out of business.

5. Education

A glaring example of failure, because of a monopoly, is the education system in the United States. Here the problem is twofold: a lack of competition to give parents a choice in the best interests of their children and an almost total inability to remove incompetent administrators, bureaucrats, and teachers because of a union in a monopoly environment. This lack of competition in education has led to the philosophy that no child should excel above another lest someone's feelings be hurt. Is there any more damaging philosophy to future wealth generation in this country than that which says we should "dumb-down" our children? Who will be hurt most if wealth generation decreases? As always, the poor. There is nothing wrong when there are differences in the abilities of children. This is a natural state. What we must learn is tolerance for differences but with the realization that everyone has the capability to make a useful, productive contribution to society. It is only when an individual does not use their talents to make a useful contribution that we should be critical.

6. Dishonesty

Theft and widespread crime are a tremendous drain on the wealth and the standard of living of a society. Unfortunately, this category is growing rapidly. Society is getting more complex, populations are growing rapidly, and there is a degradation in values in terms of respect for others, for private property, or taking responsibility for one's actions. Addiction to drugs and greater perversity add to the problem. Wealth acquired by theft, of course, makes no contribution to society and has a significant negative impact on useful productivity. Robbery, fraud, embezzlement, and bribery are forms of dishonesty that decrease wealth and decrease a society's standard of living. Empires have fallen because of a tolerance for widespread dishonesty. A society must be vigilant to promote the importance of honesty in every endeavor. Dishonesty and criminal behavior are the antitheses of **useful productivity.** The importance of honesty to the well being of the individual and to society must be taught a very young age. The missing check and balance is the need to be more diligent in our schools to promote honesty, the need to be less tolerant of dishonesty, and the need within government to espouse honesty and to serve as a good example to society.

XIV. Revitalization of the Cities

Many of the cities in the United States have declined tremendously in the past half-century. It is often argued that what is needed is a vast transfer of wealth to the cities to restore them to their former glory. But this is not a solution because wealth transfer does not create jobs, **only wealth creation creates jobs.**

The foremost and most essential need is to restore the **useful productivity** capability of cities. What is needed to do this ? Cities can be revitalized but they must have:

1. A population who understands the importance of useful productivity to the improvement of their personal well-being and understands that it is their duty to society to perform useful work.
2. A population who understands that relying on transfer of wealth from other workers leads to their own downfall.
3. A population who is willing to become educated sufficiently to learn a skill or craft that will allow them to do useful work and contribute to the useful productivity of society.
4. A city government that realizes it must create an environment in which useful productivity can flourish, meaning it must have an infrastructure in terms of efficient roads for commerce, competitively priced utility systems (power, water, sewers), a tax structure that is not a disincentive for productive individuals to remain in the city, an education system that is consistent with the need to create individuals with useful skills, a system of law and order that protects

productive individuals and productive industries, and a city government that is small and efficient as possible rather than one that is viewed as a source of employment for the well-connected or as an exchange for votes.

5. A population that realizes that crime is one of their worst enemies in the struggle to rejuvenate a city and will accept all reasonable steps to control crime.

6. A population that acknowledges that creating children is very easy but that raising them to be responsible, contributing citizens is very difficult. Changes must be made that will create an incentive to have two parents raise a child and then be responsible to raise their children to accept their societal contract.

If these conditions were to be accepted as necessary for the rebirth of a city and accepted by the population, then an opportunity is created. Investment capital and loans would then flow into the city to make good things happen. A city that would operate in this manner wouldn't have to worry about getting a handout. This kind of city would be a tremendous place to live in and invest in. It would be a place where people would live without fear and enjoy the conveniences and cultural opportunities that only a city can provide. To make it happen would take a tremendous change in mind-set. Can we learn by reason or must we only learn from experience that actions based only on taking from others is really not in our own self-interest?

XV. Improving Productivity

A statement made previously is worth repeating: **Creation of wealth creates a demand for jobs.** We increase the wealth of society by increasing individual useful productivity. We can increase individual useful productivity in a number of ways:

1. Make people who are doing useful work more productive.
2. Shift people from nonproductive work or from work having little value to useful work.
3. Get people who are doing essentially no work or even destroying wealth to become productive individuals who can make at least some contribution to society by doing useful work.
4. Use available capital more wisely.

How do we make productive people more productive? Principally by eliminating impediments that limit their productivity and allowing business and government to become more efficient. Useful productivity is increased if the cost and complexity of doing business can be reduced. There is a tendency by many people to criticize a business if its profits increase. But this is a misplaced concern. Profits from a business are the primary source of capital funds to expand or modernize and create new jobs. If profits get too high, it is a signal to other companies to enter that business. This increases the level of competition and drives excessive profits down. If criticism is to be levied, it should be on those items that increase the cost of doing business without providing a commensurate benefit.

What are some of the areas of high costs that can

make U.S. industry noncompetitive? Some of the more important of these are:

Unnecessarily complex government rules and procedures

Excessive executive and entrepreneur salaries and perks (i.e., greed)

Inefficient facilities

Restrictive work practices

High cost of utilities.

Inadequate infrastructure (roads, rail lines, airports, harbors, etc.)

Excessive taxation

High insurance costs

Excessive litigation

High cost of capital

Overly high wages and benefits

Much has been written about the chilling effect of these items on society's wealth-generating systems. A few comments may be in order.

Government has a great impact on the cost of doing business. It writes rules and regulations that often are much more complex than necessary because the rule makers are striving for perfection in the rules rather than focusing on an end result, which would be in the general public interest. Many businesses have failed because of the cost of complying with complex rules that are created by poorly written laws. Also, many government workers have a "viewpoint" problem. Their viewpoint is not necessarily to protect the public and to help business comply with necessary rules. Their attitude may be that the public and business are enemies to be harassed and punished whenever possible. Government often imposes a complex potpourri of taxes many of which foreign competitors don't have to pay. Taxes on business impose a cost that must be passed on to the consumer. Also, there seems to be little recognition of the vital importance of facilitating commerce by being helpful rather than adversarial.

Complex laws and their rules are very difficult to administer and enforce. The U.S. income tax rules are a prime example. Government workers don't understand them, the public doesn't understand them, business doesn't understand them, they are costly to comply with, and there is a great amount of noncompliance and tax cheating because of this complexity. This is the perfect example of bad law. With simpler laws, government workers could enforce them more effectively and at lower cost, and greater compliance would be obtained. With simpler laws and the privatization of many government operations, the size of government could be reduced greatly while still accomplishing all the tasks that a society expects of government.

Selecting the most competent person for a position of responsibility is most important in all aspects of life. Selecting the most competent person has two key benefits. First, it assures that responsibilities will be carried out with the most favorable impact on increasing useful productivity. Second, others always have more respect for a person with responsibility if that person is competent. This brings harmony and pride to an organization. As has been noted by the author, Laurence J. Peter, people tend to rise to their level of **incompetence** as they progress through an organization (the Peter Principle) because they strive for recognition through position rather than accomplishment. If an individual rises to his or her level of incompetence, there are three choices: 1. Leave the individual in the position to do an incompetent job, 2. Fire them, or 3. Move them to a position where they will be competent. Management often chooses the first two options to avoid suggesting they made a mistake in promoting the individual in the first place. But there should be no shame or reluctance to move a person who has risen too high, back to that person's level of competence. It is certainly better to do this for good employees rather than firing them or leaving them in a position where they are incompetent. Relocating them will maintain that person's peace of mind and ability to be useful as well as maintain the health of the organization.

XVI. The Job Loss Dilemma

What about the loss of jobs in industry and government when organizations become more efficient and do not require as many employees? Preserving inefficient or useless work does not create wealth for society. Where there is no wealth creation, there is no job creation. A useless job is the equivalent of welfare. Since people doing useless work or no work do not create wealth for society, it is in society's interest to foster a mechanism to facilitate and encourage people to accept change when jobs become outmoded. Much social unrest has occurred over the centuries as workers have understandably resisted the loss of their livelihood because economic conditions so dictated. Attempts have been made to stop technology or, in essence, stop the clock of time in order to preserve an industry that no longer makes products that consumers want or jobs that are no longer needed. These attempts always fail in the long run because the cost of maintaining work that does not generate wealth becomes such an enormous cost to society that society becomes unwilling finally to subsidize the farce.

It is an enormous challenge for society to find an efficient mechanism to facilitate the shifting of people from useless or unneeded work to something useful that will provide adequate income and dignity to those being displaced. There is no single or simple answer to this problem. Putting people who have lost their jobs on a government payroll is probably the worst possible solution because it is almost impossible, short of government bankruptcy or revolution, to eliminate a government program once established. The solution may lie with a multifaceted approach, much of which is being done today.

First is the psychological aspect of the problem,

namely the fear of losing one's job and income and the perceived stigma that society will look down on anyone who loses their job. It is most important that people be conditioned to the fact that it is in their self-interest and society's interest to change jobs when their work is becoming outmoded because of a change in technology, consumer demand, or environmental circumstances. It is in the self-interest of individuals to be alert to changing circumstances and to acquire new skills by training that will qualify themselves for work that is in demand or to seek more promising alternatives within their current skills. It is in society's interest to facilitate the training of individuals with outmoded skills, to facilitate their relocation if necessary, and to provide a safety net of income until new, useful employment can be obtained. It is also in society's interest to encourage entrepreneurs to develop new businesses and to avoid diminishing the capital available that is necessary to start new businesses or expand existing ones.

Since government should act in the long-term interests of society, it would be sensible if government programs that are aimed at maximizing the number of people doing useful work would consist of the following:

1. Emphasize by media means, the value to society and people's own self-interest of the importance of doing useful work. Because useful work is so important to the well-being of a society, it is vital that new jobs and businesses be created to provide employment for people being displaced from outmoded or inefficient businesses.

2. Set as a basic goal of public-funded education that everyone, in addition to learning general

knowledge, should develop skills that will permit them to do useful work in their lifetime.

3. Facilitate the retraining of individuals who no longer have useful or up-to-date skills.

4. Provide and maintain an unemployment insurance fund to provide temporary income to those displaced from their jobs through no fault of their own.

5. Postpone and reduce taxes for individuals who relocate to obtain employment.

6. Eliminate taxes on business profits that are reinvested in the business and thereby modernize or expand the business and create new jobs.

7. Phase out welfare for those not permanently incapacitated and instead provide supplemental income for citizens working a minimum of say, thirty-five hours a week in the private sector so they can live without welfare or other manpower intensive and uncontrollable or unaccountable bureaucratic programs. Such supplemental income programs would have to on a sliding scale to provide an encouragement to individuals to improve their situation and be verifiable to minimize cheating and double dipping as occurs now in government handout programs.

XVII. The "Free Lunch" Syndrome

It is natural for people to want bargains or the best value for their efforts. So it is somewhat natural to accept an offer by politicians to establish a new social program that will address some need or symptomatic problem in society. The politicians promise it will cost very little, but, in any case, it will be paid for mostly or entirely by someone else. It is a failing of democracy and the perceptiveness of voters that many politicians get elected by promising some favor or benefit that will be paid for by someone else. History has shown that social programs established on this premise eventually fail because costs are always much more than predicted and grow uncontrollably, and the cost of the program falls on a much broader and different spectrum of people than originally proposed. Has there ever been a government social program that truly was more successful than a mandated but privatized approach?

For example, Social Security is touted as a major government success and one can not argue with the importance of having a mechanism in place that results in retired individuals being provided for in their old age. But if saving for old age were a mandated requirement and the same amount of money that is now collected were to be invested in the private sector, the benefit to the retiree would be at least threefold from what it is now plus the retiree would have an estate to pass on to his or her heirs. The funds invested in the private sector would provide capital to businesses for the creation of jobs and new wealth and greater prosperity for the country. In contrast, the government has taken Social Security funds that should have been invested and, instead, spent them on so called "free lunch" programs. I.O.U.'s have been substituted for the spent funds that would require raising taxes to redeem them. As a result, the U.S. debt is much greater than officially disclosed. Is this debt the kind of legacy that we should pass on to our children and future generations?

It is also not surprising that the communities that tend to elect politicians promising the most handouts or "free lunches" are the ones with the poorest quality of life. This poorer state of affairs is usually blamed on the exploitation by others or not getting their fair share or bad luck or some other unfairness. However, the result is explained by basic fundamentals. A community can not thrive if it is dependent upon the work of others for its well-being. Quality of life is generated by the wealth created by the useful work of individuals and the wise application of available capital. In contrast, the promises made by many politicians often waste the money created by useful work rather than foster an environment where more useful work and wealth can be generated. So, if things don't turn out well for the "free lunch" social programs promised by politicians, and they end up being paid for by the hard working, middle class taxpayer, the voter in favor of these "free lunches" need look no further than in the mirror for the culprit who has his hand in someone else's pocketbook. There would seem to be no greater natural law in the world that would help mankind than, **"I help myself the most when I help my neighbor."** The converse, of course, is "If I steal from my neighbor (or my community or my country or from society), I am stealing from myself and my future generations."

The young are the greatest victims of the "Free Lunch Syndrome" since the "goodies" doled out by the politicians through the mechanism of debt are left for the young to pay through their future work efforts. It is surprising that the young, particularly those just entering the work force, don't scream out in horror at the monstrous burden being levied upon their future efforts.

XVIII. The Importance of Infrastructure

Infrastructure is one of those things that gets taken for granted. We know what is there, but not many people think about it or talk about it unless they find out someone wants to add to the infrastructure, such as putting a road too close to their homes or building a cellular communication tower where it will ruin their view. If you are a recluse living in the mountains, you may not need any infrastructure. But, if you're like most people trying to earn a living, infrastructure is very important. Infrastructure is something most everybody needs but not everybody wants, particularly in their backyard.

Why is infrastructure so important? Because the availability of suitable infrastructure governs where we work, where we live, and how we live. Infrastructure is vital to the generation of wealth in society, it impacts our useful productivity, and it is a major factor as to whether a society will prosper or mire in poverty. Good infrastructure allows raw materials and workers with appropriate skills to be brought to a location where something of useful value can be made and then these useful goods distributed to customers wherever they may be. Infrastructure includes facilities such as roads, rail freight, public transportation, waterways, and utilities (water, sewers, garbage, electricity, fuel, communications, etc.) that allow business and a resident population to function in a cohesive, efficient manner with civilized amenities. If an element of infrastructure is inadequate or too costly, it affects an area's suitability for business as well as the quality of life of its residents.

Business is always alert to the costs they incur because of infrastructure lest the cost of their products become uncompetitive. They seek locations with good infrastructure and may abandon locations with poor infrastructure. Employees are more productive and content when they can get to their jobs with a minimum of hassle and cost. So an adequate supply of skilled labor is more likely to be found where infrastructure and quality of life is good.

What happens when infrastructure is insufficient? Consider this situation. Suppose a road network is inadequate in a congested area with a variety of businesses. The cost to these businesses for receipt of raw materials and delivery of goods is increased because more driver time is needed, more trucks are needed, and truck operating and maintenance costs are higher. Workers waste more time getting to and from work, spend more money for travel costs, and get frustrated from their driving ordeal. Time is wasted getting to meetings and customers. At some level of inadequacy, businesses will leave for a more favorable location and new businesses will reject the area as being too congested. The impact is the same if utilities such as water, sewers, and refuse deposal cost too much. What about cities where workers may depend upon public transportation to get to their jobs? If buses or commuter trains are unreliable, costly, slow, and subject to strikes, then businesses and skilled workers will not stay if they have alternatives.

Maintaining and enhancing infrastructure is not a high priority item for most people. There is usually no constituency clamoring for better infrastructure whereas there are constituencies clamoring for special favors or enhanced social programs. Thus, in most cities, the infrastructure gets little attention and it wanes or becomes inadequate to the point that businesses leave in frustration and jobs with them. This has led to the unfortunate condition of businesses abandoning established industrial areas and moving to new locations, which soon become congested and inadequate in an ever-expanding cycle of destroying one pristine area after another. People, of course, need jobs and business must locate somewhere. It is unfortunate to continue to destroy the grandeur of nature because of the lack of attention to maintain infrastructure in areas that are best suited for business.

Infrastructure is vital to the efficient functioning of society. So how does society decide where to put it, how big to make, and how to fund it? The answer seems to be that society, in general, does a fairly good job if the decision is decided by the private sector in a competitive environment. It seems to do a pretty bad job if the decision is made in a non-competitive way through government.

Infrastructure decisions in the private sector are driven, for the most part, by a profit motive and economics. If a profit seems assured, capital funding is available, and permits are obtainable, then private enterprise usually satisfies an infrastructure demand without fuss or ado. Private enterprise most frequently provides railroads for freight, air travel, telephone/cellular/computer communications, electric power, fuel supply, and sometimes water and refuse collection. Where competition prevails, the cost of these services is about the same for all locations. Thus, the public and business tend to take it for granted that private enterprise will furnish infrastructure in a timely and adequate manner wherever there is sufficient demand and a competitive environment.

However, much of infrastructure is provided by government and that is a different story. Governments usually are the ones to provide roads, bridges, waterways, airports, commuter rail transportation, and urban bus/trolley transit. Government also provides infrastructure where demand is low (i.e., sparsely populated) or where government sponsors special projects, such as hydroelectric dams or water reservoirs and aqueducts. How are the decisions made in prioritizing the allocation of taxpayer funds for government-controlled infrastructure projects? There is no simple answer. There is no effective planning on a countrywide, statewide, or local basis that assesses infrastructure needs objectively. Who then recommends and substantiates the need for infrastructure based on economic need and the improvement of useful productivity? Unfortunately, government infrastructure decisions are generally made through the political power of individuals and through special interest group pressure.

Let's consider the question of building and maintaining roads. If enhancing useful productivity and enhancing the quality of life were a society's goal, then most road construction would take place where it would do the most good. This would be in locations where the concentration of business and workers was high but the road system was inadequate and unsafe. However, most federal money for roads is spent in locations where population and business density is sparse. Why is this? Because it's easier to build roads in less congested areas. Although, roads should be built and maintained in areas where the greatest improvement in useful productivity can be obtained, this does not happen for a number of reasons. Here are some of the factors that decide where new road projects will go:

1. The need for politicians to bring home the "bacon."

2. Local opposition to road improvements by the people who are affected directly and those who believe that improving roads will only add to additional growth and congestion.
3. It is easier to build roads in less-populated areas because it costs less and there is less opposition.
4. There is no statutory mechanism to consider the impact of road construction on improving useful productivity.
5. Improving roads is usually a low priority for politicians, particularly when there is pressure to expand social programs.
6. Many important positions in state and local transportation departments are filled on the basis of patronage. This politicizes the function and reduces the department's effectiveness and objectivity.

Road infrastructure in the United States seems to lag the need by about twenty to thirty years. This is a severe indictment of society's ability to plan for growth. Businesses continue to abandon cities because of lack of adequate infrastructure. Farming and woodland areas disappear at an alarming rate as business seeks sites that are more adequate to their needs and that will keep their costs at a competitive level.

Expenditures for infrastructure can only be made wisely when the benefits for improving useful productivity are foremost in the minds of the decision makers. Businesses will then remain where businesses should be, and farm and rural areas will be preserved for future generations. When infrastructure is adequate, useful productivity can take place and wealth generation and quality of life improvements can follow. On the other hand, countries without adequate infrastructure can not escape a subsistence existence and countries that let their infrastructure deteriorate will fall by the wayside and suffer a loss in quality of life.

XIX. The "Don't Rock the Boat" Syndrome

It is a characteristic of mankind to avoid self-criticism or blame. After all, blame often results in punishment, so it is natural for people to take extraordinary steps to cover up a mistake or to deny fault or to find some way of blaming others when something goes wrong. Anyone who has raised children can probably remember the time when they were young and something went awry, then either "nobody did it" or the "baby did it." Avoiding blame is something ingrained in us at an early age. In some societies, it is especially bad to have it revealed that you had made a mistake as that might make you lose face (i.e., self-esteem) to the point that the individual might even take his or her own life.

This ingrained tendency in mankind to avoid blame has unfortunate consequences on the useful productivity of society. History is replete with an enormous number of examples of instances in which businesses have suffered or societies have suffered because no one had the courage to admit they were on the wrong path or that a mistake had been made. Think of the recent example that rated a rather small headline in the newspaper. To wit, "Internal Revenue Service abandons an effort to computerize the department after having spent $3 billion." Now surely someone realized early on that such a vast undertaking to recomputerize a huge system was bound to fail. Surely someone alerted their managers that things were not going well. However, if a halt was called when this was apparent, they would have had unused funding and someone would have appeared to make a mistake. What were the consequences to the IRS to continue to waste funds for this project? Did anyone get fired? Did anyone get demoted? Surely not the top managers who had the ultimate responsibility to use the funds wisely. The cover-up seems to have gone well because there were no ramifications of this enormous waste of funds that otherwise could have been used for something productive.

Government is particularly prone to cover-ups because it is a monopoly with little oversight and there is little or no penalty for poor decisions or poor work. However, business is not immune to hiding mistakes. Businesses can cover up mistakes until that time when it hits the profit line and then some competitor takes advantage of their weakened condition. It is interesting that the recent downsizing of much of U.S. industry is a result of not facing reality sooner. The attitude was "Don't rock the boat." Things are going OK. We're comfortable. So maybe we're inefficient. Maybe we have too many employees and maybe we have too many employees who were not suited for the work that they were doing. But when things get tough, niceties have to go and many loyal employees have found themselves without jobs as companies try to reduce costs. Wouldn't it have been better for management to have been alert to the changing directions of the economy and technology? Wouldn't it have been better to downsize slowly and move people around where possible? A tremendous amount of loyalty has been lost by the U.S. worker because of the traumatic way that downsizing was handled even though it was absolutely necessary.

It is natural for mankind to make mistakes. Making mistakes is a primary way in which we learn. A mistake is usually serious only when it is ignored or there is a cover-up to avoid revealing that a mistake has been made.

How do we change society's view of mistakes? It is

59

most important to reduce the consequences of revealing a mistake early, before it has done harm and increasing the penalty when there is a cover-up or the mistake is ignored. Surely, the least that should happen is termination of work for any individuals who haven't the courage to admit a mistake has been made that has serious consequences. A different mind set is needed. It is childish to blame someone else for our mistake. It shows lack of truthfulness, lack of responsibility for one's actions, and lack of honor. On the other hand, when someone, either in business or in government or in society in general, makes a mistake but owns up to as soon as it is evident that a mistake has been made, they should receive leniency. Admitting to mistakes is something to be encouraged. It is healthy. It is good for the soul. It allows an individual to accept reality.

Think of how history could have been changed if people had the courage to admit their mistakes. In World War I, millions had to die for nationalism and past historic injustices. What would have happened if Kaiser Wilhelm II had the courage to admit that the needless slaughter of innocents was not justified and negotiated for a truce. Instead he held fast and when his side lost, he hid to save himself. How sad. What about the Civil War? Each side, with its self-righteous attitude, was unwilling to compromise. Was the result worth it? Wouldn't the same result have occurred because economics was forcing change? History tells us of the fanatics that inflamed emotions on both sides until war was inevitable. The trouble with fanatics is that their arguments for change are not sufficient to convince rational people. If the arguments were sound, the change would occur peaceably. Thus, fanatics often take matters to extremes to obtain change by force. Unfortunately, fanatics are usually wrong, but they seldom will admit to their errors after the damage has been done.

Maybe we need an effort to get people to admit that they make mistakes once in a while and that it is OK to make mistakes. It would be cathartic. It would be a breath of fresh air. Maybe lawyers might even stop lying for their clients in court. Well, maybe not.

XX. Population Growth

Some people say that population must grow in order to create a continuing demand for goods and services and jobs. Obviously, more population can mean more demand for goods and services. But is population growth the only way we can keep people gainfully employed? Absolutely not. There are two ways to create a demand for goods and services and, in turn, a demand for jobs. One, of course, is by population growth. The second is to increase the wealth-generating capability of the existing population so they can afford the goods and services that would improve their quality of life. The problems facing the world because of escalating population growth are so great that focus must be shifted to the second option as a means of improving the economy of the world.

Rapid population growth is a primary cause of increasing environmental problems in the world. What is the primary cause of world deforestation? Rapid population growth. What is the primary cause of increasing pollution of the oceans, the air, and the land in spite of efforts to enact and enforce rigid environmental rules? Rapid population growth. What is the cause of a diminishing quality of life in much of the world? Rapid population growth. Unbridled population growth has the potential for destroying the means for many living things to survive on this planet. Any action to solve environmental or economic problems that does not recognize excessive population growth as an underlying problem will not succeed.

Rapid population growth and the number of poor in a society tend to go hand in hand. The majority of the people in the world today are poor. That is to say, they do not have the capability to produce more than their basic needs for survival. These individuals usually do not have the skills, resources, or facilities to be sufficiently productive to create wealth through **useful productivity.** They have insufficient, disposable income from their own productivity to exchange for the productivity of someone else. The poor in the world represent a tremendous potential demand for goods and services if they can become usefully productive so they have disposable income of their own making. Providing long-term welfare to the poor is not a way to make the poor productive and become contributing members of society. Although it is a humane thing to do, welfare makes people dependent on others when it is available on a long-term basis. The bottom line is that excessive population growth and the number of poor in the world will not diminish by rational means unless we have an economic system whereby individuals understand that they must be usefully productive and there is the wherewithal for this to happen. If mankind will not act rationally to solve this problem, then "Mother Nature" eventually will do so in her usual cruel and dispassionate way without regard for human life.

If mankind, in toto, were always able to act rationally and sensibly, only those children would be conceived whom parents knew they could care for, and love and raise to be responsible citizens. But when mankind acts without responsibility for their actions, then children are often brought into the world to survive by any means possible, with or without any concern for others. Not only are these children often condemned to a hell on earth, but they inflict their unhappiness and dissatisfaction on others with whom they come in contact. Instead of being an asset to society, these children, born of self-gratification and irresponsibility, wreak havoc through all kinds of evil as they seek revenge for their lot in life. Is there any

63

greater negative impact upon society than to bring a child recklessly into a life in which that child is condemned to survive only by destroying others or their livelihoods?

XXI. Verification of the "Useful Productivity" Principle

Since 1990, computer systems have been revolutionizing the conduct of business and the development of new products and technology. A computer does clerical tasks almost instantly, permits worldwide access to information, and tackles very complex calculations and evaluations that would have been impossible years ago. In addition, communications have improved tremendously through the medium of the computer internet, cellular telephones, and satellite television. As a result, a paradigm shift has occurred, which has had a tremendous impact on useful productivity and the nature of the work force. Radical changes in business staffing and organization have taken place where competition and free enterprise exist. Secretaries, who used to handle the work of one person, can now take care of ten and are still more productive. Clerical positions have been eliminated or reduced greatly. Middle manager positions have been reduced since the information they would laboriously gather and analyze is now consolidated and analyzed by computer systems. New ideas or concepts that used to take months to develop are now done in days. Technology design and development has increased by an order of magnitude in numbers and implementation. Control of machinery and complex systems is now handled by computer, so fewer operators are needed. Business transactions take place around the clock and around the world at dazzling speeds. The list goes on and on.

The initial impact of computerization and improved communications in the U.S. was a loss of jobs in the private sector. Government wisely kept their hands off, even though there were many pleas for job preservation. What has happened? The higher useful productivity brought about by computers and improved communications has resulted in a major increase in the total wealth of the United States. This greater wealth has caused a substantial increase in job demand. In 1998, unemployment was at an all-time low and anyone with adequate work skills could get a good job.

In a very short time period, increased useful productivity produced wealth and, in turn, the increased wealth created new jobs. Even tax revenue to the U.S. Government increased to the point that there is a budget surplus (but by using money taken from Social Security collections) for the first time in decades. Can government take any credit for this amazing period of growth and wealth? The answer is no, except that government did not interfere in the marketplace nor did it do anything that would have destabilized the currency. The advent of computers and radically improved communications have thus verified that an increase in useful productivity produced wealth and that increase produced an overall increase in jobs.

Unfortunately, there is a downside. Computers permit the more educated and the more skilled individuals in the workplace to accomplish much more, to draw more readily on the skills of others, and to take advantage of instantly available knowledge and communications. People with these skills are prospering, and there are more jobs available for them than can be filled. The less skilled, of those who have lost their jobs, often find it necessary to take a lower-paying job unless they have the ability to understand and participate in this paradigm shift. The unskilled rarely find new, high-paying jobs since many of the repetitive manufacturing jobs that they used to hold have gone to lower-wage scale countries. Thus, the unskilled are not benefitting significantly from the computer revolution, except that there is less unemployment. Just at the time when this major technological change was taking place in U.S. society, the U.S. educational system was producing a much less skilled work force than in previous generations. A recent study indicates that the U.S. is near the bottom of the list in the proficiency of its students for mathematical and science skills and knowledge. No doubt, a similar survey would surely show that U.S. students are also deficient, compared to other countries, in language skills, knowledge of history, economics, and other skills important to the continued economic success of the United States.

What will be the outcome of this apparent dichotomy of increased productivity from computers versus the poorer educational skills of students? For one, it means that the income of the more highly educated and more skilled will continue to grow and outdistance the income of the less educated and skilled (unless the government implements more wealth transfer). But it also means the less educated will be put into positions of responsibility and may not perform well, thus leading to costly business errors or more accidents. For the long term, the outlook is grim. The United States may fall from its number one economic position and Asia and Europe (except socialistic France) may rise to economic ascendancy. This outcome is inevitable unless the United States fosters competition among schools and gives free rein to an educational system that is now stifled by government bureaucracy and a monopoly union.

XXII. Conclusion

Mankind always has choices in the quest for survival and to improve the quality of life. One choice is to act selfishly and let the emotions of greed, envy, and self-gratification govern daily actions, with little or no concern for others. Throughout history, individuals and entire societies have sought personal gain by taking from others through any means, no matter how unfair or horrible. This is not a good choice because the inevitable outcome is conflict, suffering, and degradation of all society, with the aggressor eventually always losing.

An alternative approach is to foster a system whereby each individual is encouraged and nurtured to use his or her inherent natural abilities to generate a useful product or service to society. If we increase the useful productivity of the individual, then we increase the wealth-generating capability of that individual, which, in turn, generates wealth for society, creates jobs, and establishes an environment where the individual can live in harmony with his fellow man and the natural environment.

True freedom for an individual comes about when he or she has the skills to be usefully productive and the opportunity exists for the individual to use those skills. On the other hand, we take away people's freedom and make them slaves when they are given their needs for survival through welfare or a useless job. It is one thing to help someone when they are in temporary difficulty, but useless work condemns them to a dependent existence that they will resent and that will turn them against society.

Societies make their own choices as to whether the society will flourish in wealth or wallow in poverty. A so-

68

ciety chooses wealth when there is useful productivity, when individuals are educated up to their ability, when honesty is the norm, and when parents accept the responsibility to make their children useful members of society. A society chooses poverty when they look to government to satisfy their daily needs, when they consider education a waste of time, when there is no respect for personal property or individual honesty, and when raising children to be useful members of society has little priority.

The world is complex and most people do not like to deal with complexity or to consider issues objectively. They want simple answers to complex issues. There are many glib demagogues who are ready to offer "free lunch" or simple solutions. This treatise suggests some basic considerations for judging the promises of the glib. Are they offering a program that will lead to future wealth or poverty? As stated earlier, **"mankind learns by experience, not by reason."** Nevertheless, we can reduce the bad experiences if we try to reason and not just follow the blind paths of nationalism or fanaticism or the "free lunch" offerings.

The world is entering a new era of instant global information and ever-expanding high technology. There is a part that everyone can fill in this evolving society that will allow them to lead satisfying lives. Societies will prosper where work is based on **"useful productivity."** Without this approach, society can expect greater disparity between the "haves" and the "have nots." Disastrous social conflict could be inevitable. As always, there are radical groups and self-interest groups that would like to ignite social conflict or retain the status quo. Wouldn't it be better to try reasoning and logic to guide us before we reach the conflict stage? Let us hope so, for our children's sake and the world's sake.